THE ASSASSINATION OF PRESIDENT
JOHN F. KENNEDY

BY WIL MARA

FRANKLIN WATTS®
An imprint of Scholastic Inc.

Content Consultant
James Marten, PhD
Professor and Chair, History Department
Marquette University
Milwaukee, Wisconsin

Library of Congress Cataloging-in-Publication Data
Mara, Wil.
 The assassination of President John F. Kennedy / by Wil Mara.
    pages cm
 Includes bibliographical references and index.
 ISBN 978-0-531-20999-8 (library binding : alk. paper) –
 ISBN 978-0-531-21041-3 (pbk. : alk. paper)
1. Kennedy, John F. (John Fitzgerald), 1917–1963–Assassination–
Juvenile literature. I. Title.
 E842.Z9M36 2015
 973.922092–dc23   2014049201

TABLE of CONTENTS

INTRODUCTION

THE ASSASSINATION OF PRESIDENT JOHN FITZGERALD KENNEDY in November 1963 was one of the most devastating events in the history of the United States. Many decades later, there are few who do not recall—usually with uncommon clarity—where they were and what they were doing when they first heard the news.

"I was in college, in class," said one woman who lived on the East Coast at the time and is now a retired computer technician, "and the announcement came over the PA system that the president had been killed. We were all stunned. My professor had us observe a moment of silence, then we were sent home for the day."[1] A man who lived in Kansas remembered, "I was sitting in the barbershop having my hair cut, and the report came over the radio. We just sat there in disbelief. A woman from the diner next door came in and asked if we'd heard. She was crying and holding a handful of tissues."[2] And best-selling author Dominick Dunne remembered, "We were in the conference room in the executive suite at Four Star . . . six men, maybe eight, talking seriously. . . . A wonderful woman named Gladys Benito . . . walked into the serious session without knocking first and said, 'The President has just been shot.' It was a surreal moment. For a very long instant, we all stared at Gladys and did not speak, trying to absorb what she had just said. What had been so terribly important a moment before wasn't important anymore."[3]

Many schools and businesses in America closed that day—a Friday—out of respect for their fallen leader. The only facet of society that became more mobilized was the media. Millions of people remained in their homes that weekend, following along with each report as hundreds of writers and photographers descended upon Dallas, Texas—the scene of the crime—to cover what was shaping up to be The Story of the Century.

President John Kennedy's family stands outside the church after Kennedy's funeral on November 25, 1963.

Abraham Lincoln
Died: April 1865

James Garfield
Died: September 1881

William McKinley
Died: September 1901

Prior to Kennedy's assassination, three other U.S. presidents had been killed while in office: Abraham Lincoln in April 1865, James Garfield in September 1881, and William McKinley in September 1901. Before McKinley's death—as difficult as it may be to believe today—presidents had very little security around them. In fact, there was a time when an ordinary citizen could walk into the White House and request to see the president whenever he or she wished. Lincoln, for example, received unscheduled visitors fairly frequently. The Secret Service had been created by Lincoln (somewhat ironically, on the day before his own assassination), but only for the purpose of investigating the then-growing crime of counterfeiting. It did not yet play a role in presidential security. Throughout the nation's history, presidents were sometimes accompanied by guards of one type or another, often military personnel. But a determined assassin could still get within range of his target. When President McKinley was shot, for example, he was attending a world's fair in Buffalo, New York, along with a small protective cordon of guards. In spite of this protection, a disgruntled unemployed factory worker was able to move within a few feet of McKinley and shoot him point-blank with a pistol wrapped in a handkerchief. Following McKinley's death, Congress requested that the Secret Service formally begin protecting the president. From then on, while other presidents were targeted by assassins, none were killed—until November 22, 1963.

This book presents the best-known facts and numerous reasonable perspectives concerning the assassination of President Kennedy. It is doubtful that every piece of the puzzle will ever be uncovered and, thus, the picture ever made truly complete. Some of the evidence will probably remain forever shrouded in mystery. We know where Kennedy was when he was killed. We know who was with him. We know the extent of his wounds. And we know who was eventually captured in connection with his murder. But many other questions remain. Did the suspected killer act alone, or was he part of a greater conspiracy? Was the man who killed the prime suspect two days after the assassination also part of the conspiracy? If there was, in fact, a conspiracy, what was its purpose, and who

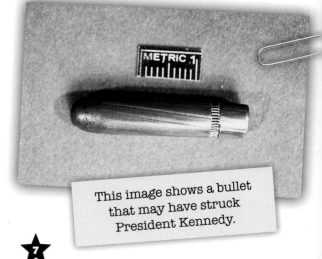

This image shows a bullet that may have struck President Kennedy.

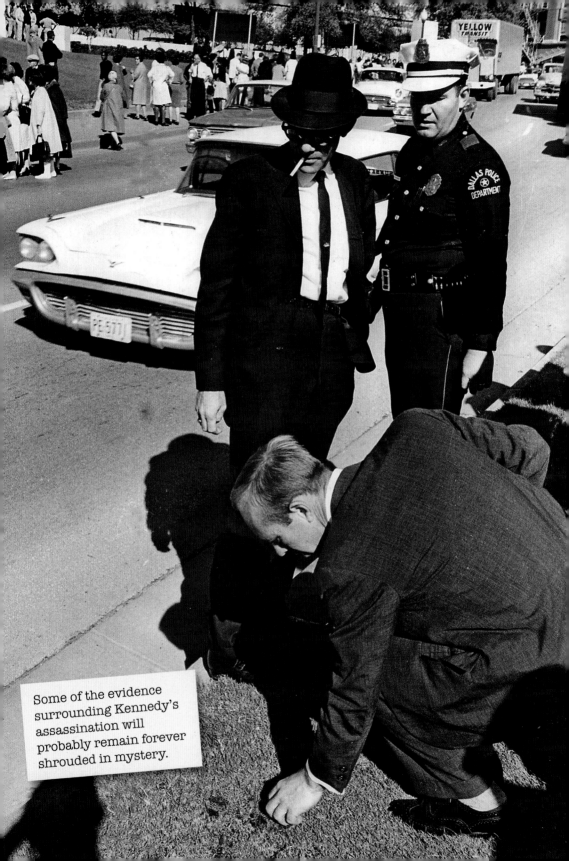

Some of the evidence surrounding Kennedy's assassination will probably remain forever shrouded in mystery.

else took part in it? And if the president's alleged killer was instead acting purely of his own accord, what motivated him to commit such a horrendous crime in the first place? What kind of man was he? And how did he manage to get away with it when the president was being protected by one of the most elite security forces in the world?

Among conspiracy buffs and amateur historians, the events surrounding the Kennedy assassination are some of the most hotly contested topics in history. This book is far from the only one that touches on the subject; there are literally hundreds. The objective here is to present the facts that are known, then offer information based on the many theories about what is not known. The question of who else may have been involved—forgetting about how these people came together, the operational plot they assembled, and how they managed to evade justice afterward—has in itself spurred a great deal of passionate debate.

It is important to remember that something more than a president's life was lost that day, something difficult to identify with precision. Helen Thomas, the famed White House correspondent from United Press International, put it well when she said, "It was a transforming moment for America because we lost hope. Every president who succeeded Kennedy, they all had good points and bad points. But the legacy of hope died with him. You never had that sense again that we were moving forward, that we could do things."[4] The nation that existed before that day certainly was not the one that existed after.

CHAPTER ONE

NOVEMBER 22, 1963

There are many conflicting theories about what exactly happened in Dallas on the day of President Kennedy's assassination. What is presented in this chapter is the most plausible version of events based on known facts, eyewitness accounts, investigative findings, and reasonable assumptions.

A NEW DAY BEGINS

It was still dark in the Texas suburb of Irving when Lee Harvey Oswald was woken by his wife, Marina. They had been married less than two years, yet the relationship was already fraught with difficulty. They had two beautiful young daughters, Rachel and June, but they now lived apart most of the time. Marina and the children had moved in with a friend, and Lee had rented a room about 13 miles (21 kilometers) away so he could be closer to his job in Dallas. The family still saw each other frequently, however, and Lee had asked Marina many times over the previous few months if they could get back together for good. Weary of his unpredictable moods and

Lee Harvey Oswald left his family's home in Irving, Texas, early on November 22, 1963.

occasional outbursts of violence, she was hesitant. When they saw each other, they still argued and fought. Nothing had changed.

Through her sleepiness, Marina heard Lee say that he was leaving some money behind. "Take it and buy everything you and Junie and Rachel need," he told her.[1] This was very odd, as he was usually tight with the little money he managed to earn. He was often unemployed, and when he found a job, he didn't usually keep it for long. In spite of this uncharacteristic flash of generosity, Marina did not reply. Stranger still was the fact that Lee took off his wedding ring and placed it in a teacup just before heading out. Marina would not notice this until much later in the day.

About an hour later, in a Fort Worth hotel room about 30 miles (48.2 km) from Irving, John Fitzgerald Kennedy, the 35th president of the United States, was just waking up. Fort Worth was one stop among many on Kennedy's current campaign tour. He did not love the process of campaigning, but 1964 would be an election year, and he needed to increase his popularity in Texas. Texas was a mostly Republican state, and Kennedy was a Democrat. He was wildly popular in other parts of the nation, though. He was tall, slender, and handsome, and he possessed a likable, easygoing manner. There was also his age. In 1960, at 43 years old, he had become the youngest man ever elected president. This delighted many voters after a generation of "old-man presidents" ending with

Kennedy shakes a young man's hand during his first presidential campaign in 1960.

NOT A WELL MAN

Kennedy's youthful aura was something of a myth, as he was frequently ill throughout his life. As a child, he spent more than two months in a hospital with scarlet fever. He also had an abnormally severe case of chicken pox and numerous inner-ear infections. He suffered appendicitis at the age of 13, and the resulting surgery kept him bedridden for a long period. During his first year of high school, he had numerous flulike colds, made worse by the fact that he never seemed to put on much weight. In his early twenties, he began having trouble with both his back and his digestive system. He eventually had a back operation that once again required a great deal of bed rest. He would experience excruciating back pain throughout his life. Long after his death, when many of his medical records were revealed to the public, it was learned that he had Addison's disease, which occurs when the adrenal glands fail to produce certain hormones. In spite of all this, he managed to conceal his suffering from the public and maintain an image of healthy energy.

Kennedy (center) visited Fort Worth, Texas, before moving on to Dallas.

Kennedy's predecessor, Dwight D. Eisenhower, who was in his early seventies when he left office. As Kennedy got out of bed that morning, he was reminded that he had to give a speech in Fort Worth, then make a short flight to Dallas to give another.

A PACKAGE OF CURTAIN RODS

Around the time the president was getting ready for his busy day, Lee Harvey Oswald was sitting in the passenger seat of a friend's car, on his way to work. Both men worked at the Texas School Book Depository in downtown Dallas. During the drive, the friend noticed a package Oswald had put in the back seat—long and thin, slightly wider at one end, and wrapped in brown paper. Oswald told him it contained curtain rods. When they arrived at the book depository, Oswald grabbed the package and hurried off.

The president's plane landed at Dallas's Love Field at approximately 11:40 a.m., and a huge crowd was waiting to welcome him. His wife, whose name was Jacqueline but was usually referred to as "Jackie," appeared first and received enthusiastic applause. Like her husband, she was young and attractive, and she had many fans of her own. To the crowd's delight, the Kennedys came over to say hello and shake hands. The tarmac was still wet from the rain that had fallen earlier, but the skies had since cleared. It was turning out to be a wonderful day.

A crowd of people greet John and Jackie Kennedy at Love Field in Dallas.

Around this time, Oswald was standing by the open shaft of a freight elevator on the fifth floor of the book depository. As the elevator car came by on its way down, Oswald saw that a few of his co-workers were on it. He asked them to close the gate after they got off at the bottom. If the gate wasn't closed, a safety feature on the car would prevent it from going up again. These co-workers did not have a very favorable opinion of Oswald. He rarely spoke to anyone, and when he did he came across as moody and arrogant. When they reached the bottom, none of them bothered to close the gate for him.

The Kennedys got into their limousine a few minutes before noon. The limo was part of a long line of vehicles that made up the president's motorcade. Other notable people riding in the motorcade included Vice President Lyndon Baines Johnson and Texas senator Ralph Yarborough. There were Secret Service agents everywhere, as well as dozens of Dallas police officers. Protection was of prime importance on this trip, as Kennedy had received numerous threats from radical organizations and unstable individuals in the weeks beforehand. Kennedy had even said earlier in the day, "It would not be a very difficult job to shoot the president of the United States. All you'd have to do is get up in a high building with a high-powered rifle with a telescopic sight, and there's nothing anybody could do."[2]

The motorcade pulled out of Love Field at noon and headed for downtown Dallas. Riding with the president and first lady was

The Kennedys sit in the back of the open convertible in Dallas. Texas Governor John Connally (bottom right) is in front of them.

Governor John Connally and his wife, Nellie. The custom-built limousine had three rows of seats—front, middle, and back. A Secret Service agent was in the front with the driver, the Connallys were in the middle, and the Kennedys were in the back. The limo could also be fitted with a clear-plastic "bubble" instead of its normal hardtop roof. But because the weather was nice, Kennedy had requested that the bubble be left off the vehicle. There were also running boards on either side of the car where Secret Service agents could stand while it rolled along. Kennedy did not like this and asked that the agents stay clear. He did not want to feel too isolated from ordinary citizens.

The Texas School Book Depository is a seven-story building in downtown Dallas.

THE SIXTH FLOOR

Around the time the presidential motorcade left Love Field, one of Oswald's co-workers went up to the sixth floor of the book depository to get a pack of cigarettes. While there, he noticed Oswald walking around with a clipboard. It seemed strange that Oswald would be working during lunch. When he asked Oswald if he'd be going down to the lunchroom, Oswald said no. The man thought nothing more of it and took the elevator back down. A few minutes later, another co-worker came to the sixth floor. He had heard that President Kennedy would be passing by, and he wanted to have a good view. He did not see Oswald during this time. He sat down by one of the windows and ate his lunch, hoping some of his friends would join him. When none did, he finished eating and

Crowds lined the streets of Dallas to see the president drive by.

went to the fifth floor instead. There he found two other co-workers. They went together to the southeastern corner of the building and waited for the president to pass below them.

The motorcade turned onto Main Street in downtown Dallas around 12:20 p.m. All along the journey from Love Field, there had been thousands of people waving and cheering. Now the crowds were thicker than ever, spilling into the streets and slowing the motorcade's progress. The Kennedys did not mind. They were delighted by the warm welcome. As the motorcade crawled through the hallway of tall buildings, Kennedy and his wife smiled and waved back to their admirers.

The motorcade finally reached the end of Main Street at 12:29 and entered Dealey Plaza. From a bird's-eye view, the plaza formed

The motorcade entered Dealey Plaza and turned right onto Houston Street, then a quick left onto Elm—where three shots rang out just seconds later.

a triangular shape as three main roads in downtown Dallas came together at a point, then ran under a long railroad bridge before continuing onto the Stemmons Freeway. The motorcade made a right turn from Main onto Houston, then a left onto Elm. The crowd was much thinner here, but the mood was just as frenzied. People were still calling for the president and first lady to wave to them or to turn in their direction so they could take photos.

One man looked up toward the book depository and saw the workers who were watching the president from the windows. He took particular note of a figure visible through a sixth-floor window on the far east side of the building. But no one else in Dealey Plaza took any notice of the man on the sixth floor. All eyes were on the president and his wife. Many people were clicking pictures or recording films—creating images that, in light of what happened next, would be analyzed exhaustively in the years ahead. In another moment of irony, Nellie Connally turned to Kennedy and said, "Mr. President, they can't make you believe now that there are not some in Dallas who love you and appreciate you, can they?" The president, in the last utterance of his life, smiled and replied, "No, they sure can't."[3] The limo began down Elm Street around 12:30 with the president and first lady still waving and smiling.

Then it began.

Employees at the Texas School Book Depository watch out the window as Kennedy's motorcade drives into Dealey Plaza.

EIGHT SECONDS THAT CHANGED AMERICA

The first shot cut through the din like a firecracker. Many thought it was just that—a prank pulled by some kid to taunt the security team or by some lunatic looking to scare the president. Others said they initially thought the sound was a car or motorcycle backfiring. Still others thought it was a gun firing a military salute in the president's honor. A few people, however, knew exactly what it was—and Governor Connally, sitting directly in front of the president, was one of them. An experienced hunter, he was very familiar with the sound of a rifle shot. Fearing that this was the beginning of an

Police officers keep an eye on the crowd as the Connallys (left) and Kennedys (right) enter Dealey Plaza.

President Kennedy can be seen slumping over in the back of the open limousine just after being shot.

assault, he said, "Oh no, no, no ..."[4] He looked back to see if the president or first lady had been hit, but the first bullet had missed its mark and instead struck a nearby curb.

The second shot came less than four seconds later, and it erased all remaining doubts. President Kennedy's hands went to his neck, his elbows up, as the bullet entered high on his back and exited at the base of his throat. It continued through the seat in front of him and struck Governor Connally in the back, driving him downward. Connally cried out, "My God, they're going to kill us all!"[5] Then his wife pulled him down for protection and covered his head with her own.

Agent Clinton Hill climbs onto the back of the moving limousine to protect the first lady.

Jackie Kennedy turned to her husband, who had a pained expression on his face and was unable to speak. Doctors would later theorize that he likely would have survived the attack if this first wound had been the only one. Elsewhere in Dealey Plaza, as people began to realize what was happening, they fled or dropped to the ground. Meanwhile, a few Secret Service agents were running toward the president to protect him from further harm. Tragically, they would not reach him in time.

The third, final, and fatal shot arrived eight seconds after the first. It entered the president's head on the top right side, fragmenting large pieces of his scalp, skull, and brain tissue. For all practical purposes, he was killed at this moment. Even if he had received immediate medical attention, he would not have survived. His body went limp and slumped toward his wife, who cried out, "Oh no, no, no. Oh my God, they have shot my husband. I love you, Jack."[6] Then, in an act she would later claim to not remember, Jackie climbed onto the trunk of the limousine, possibly to retrieve some part of her husband's skull that had been blown away by the fatal bullet. A Secret Service agent who had reached the car by this point forced Jackie back into the seat in case more shots came. The driver was then ordered to head for the nearest hospital, Parkland Memorial. As the limousine sped off, Jackie cradled the president in her lap. It was like a scene out of a horror movie, with blood everywhere. The first lady would later say, "I kept holding the top of his head down ... but I knew he was dead."[7]

GROWING CHAOS

Back in Dealey Plaza, the scene was sheer mayhem. People continued seeking cover, unsure if more shots would come. Many were already claiming to have seen a rifle barrel sticking out of the sixth-floor window of the book depository, leading police and Secret Service agents to swarm the building. The three workers who had been watching the motorcade from the fifth-floor window clearly heard a rifle being fired above them, as well as the distinct sound of cartridge shells hitting the floor. One of the three men would even find ceiling dust in his hair from the shock waves caused by each shot. But who was up there? Who had pulled the

Spectators stay low to the ground as photographers rush to snap photos seconds after the shooting.

trigger? While authorities mulled over this question, journalists were already reporting the incident, saying that they believed the president had been struck, but they did not yet know if his wounds were serious.

Inside the book depository, one Dallas police officer asked the building's superintendent to bring him to the sixth floor. However, the elevator would not come down—the gate was open. When the superintendent called up for someone to close the gate, he received no reply. The officer went to the nearest staircase instead. As he reached the second floor, the officer noticed through a little window in the staircase door that a man was walking away from him. He pulled the door open, pointed his revolver at the man, and ordered him to come over to him. It was Oswald. He did not appear to be nervous or frightened, and in fact seemed perfectly calm. The officer asked the superintendent if he knew who the man was. The super said that he did and that Oswald worked in the building. Satisfied, the officer went back to the stairs and continued up. Oswald was seen again a few moments later—this time on the first floor—by one of his co-workers, who noticed he had a bottle of Coca-Cola in his hand. She said something to him, but he only mumbled a reply. A few moments later, Oswald walked out the front entrance of the building.

The president's limousine arrived at Parkland Memorial Hospital at around 12:35, and two gurneys were rolled out—one for Governor Connally and one for President Kennedy. Jackie refused

AMBULANCES ONLY

Secret Service agents replaced the roof on the president's limousine soon after reaching the hospital.

to let go of her husband's body, despite gentle urgings from the Secret Service. "You know he's dead. Let me alone," she told them.[8] Then one of the agents realized the reason for her reluctance—she didn't want anyone to see her husband in such a gruesome state. The agent took off his coat and covered the president's head and upper body, and Jackie finally let him go. President Kennedy was then lifted onto the waiting gurney and wheeled inside.

At 12:45, Oswald calmly stepped into a taxi not far from Dealey Plaza. The cab driver did not yet know about the shooting, but he'd heard some of the noise coming from the plaza and asked Oswald about it. When Oswald didn't respond, the driver figured he just wasn't the friendly type. He ended up dropping off Oswald near the room he had been renting for the last few months. The woman who owned the house said something as Oswald came in, but he didn't reply to her, either. This did not surprise her, as she had already decided he was a fairly rude individual. Oswald went into his room, quickly retrieved a handgun and a jacket, and left again.

NOT ONE DEATH, BUT TWO

Back at Parkland, doctors worked frantically on the president. This was not so much because they believed he could be saved, but because they had to try. His respiratory system was still functioning to a small degree, trying to catch a breath. Every now and then

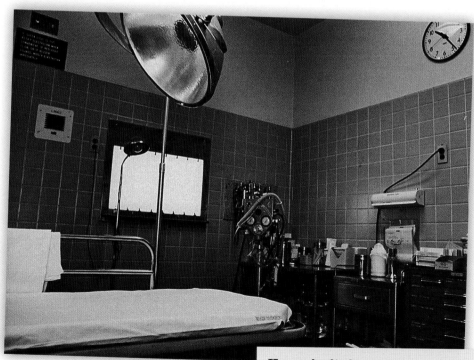

Kennedy died in a trauma room in Parkland Hospital.

Reporters rushed to Parkland Hospital to learn more about the president's condition.

there was a slight flicker of a heartbeat. But the doctors knew these were all automatic functions, indications of a body trying to sustain itself. The reality was that Kennedy had lost too much blood and that a large section of his brain was gone. At 1:00 p.m., with no remaining pulse, he was officially declared dead.

Less than fifteen minutes later, Oswald was walking through the neighborhood near his rented room when a police car pulled up alongside him. Oswald stopped, and the officer lowered his passenger-side window. The officer was on the lookout for a man who matched Oswald's description. Oswald went to the side of the car and spoke to the officer through the open window for a

Police and Secret Service agents had to contend with huge crowds outside the hospital.

moment. To anyone passing by, it would have appeared as though they were having a perfectly ordinary, even friendly, conversation. Then the officer, whose name was J. D. Tippit, sensed something suspicious about Oswald. He got out of the car and began walking around the front. As he drew closer, Oswald pulled out his handgun and fired multiple times. Tippit doubled over and fell to the ground. Before leaving the scene, Oswald went back and fired one more round into the officer's head. Then he calmly walked away. He would not be able to escape so easily from this shooting, however—several witnesses had seen everything.

Oswald also shot a Dallas policeman with a handgun that day.

THE ZAPRUDER FILM

The most famous, and certainly most horrific, moving images of the Kennedy assassination were taken by a man named Abraham Zapruder. Zapruder, a Ukrainian immigrant and clothing manufacturer, was a Democrat and great admirer of President Kennedy.

He brought his movie camera to Dealey Plaza that day, then positioned himself on a high marble pedestal west of Elm Street. This gave him an excellent view of the motorcade route. He shot just under 30 seconds of film before realizing what had happened. The film was developed later that afternoon, and Zapruder gave copies to the Secret Service for investigative purposes. Two days later, he sold the rights to the film to *Life* magazine under the condition that they not use frame 313, which contained the grisly fatal headshot. Then he gave 25 percent of the money to the widow of Officer J. D. Tippit. In spite of Zapruder's demand that frame 313 never be shown, the full film was leaked to the public in 1975.

Word spread quickly about the shooting of Officer Tippit, and a massive manhunt followed. It did not take long for the authorities to realize that the description of Tippit's killer and that of the president's were a match. Meanwhile, news of the president's confirmed death was being relayed around the world.

At 1:22, investigators at the book depository found a rifle and empty shell cartridges on the sixth floor. The rifle had been hidden among some boxes, but the cartridges were lying in plain view near the sniper's window. Finger and palm prints found on the rifle and in the general area would eventually be matched to those of Lee Harvey Oswald.

THE SUSPECT IS CAPTURED

Shortly after 1:30, the manager of a shoe store in Dallas's business district saw a small man with short, dark hair step into the foyer of the store and remain there for a moment with his back to the street while police cars zoomed past; then the man continued on his way. The manager had been following the day's horrible news on the radio, and he had heard a description of the suspect. When he stepped out onto the sidewalk, he saw the man moving at a hurried pace and ducking into a movie theater. The manager ran to the theater and talked with two of its employees. They all agreed that the man was acting suspiciously, and by 1:45 the police had been alerted.

Five minutes later, four officers arrived on the scene and went into the theater. It took them a moment to locate Oswald in the

Vice President Lyndon Johnson (center) is sworn in as president with Jacqueline Kennedy (right) by his side.

darkness. When they did, Oswald reached for his gun and tried to fight back. He never got the chance to fire it, as the four officers got him under control and led him away. His last words as a free man were, "Well, it's all over now."[9]

On Air Force One—the presidential airplane—Vice President Lyndon Baines Johnson waited in the cabin with his wife on one side and Jackie Kennedy on the other. At 2:38, Sarah Hughes, a judge and longtime friend of Johnson's, swore him in as America's 36th president. Then they started back to Washington, with the body of John Fitzgerald Kennedy on board.

CHAPTER TWO

A GARDEN OF OPPORTUNITY

What circumstances had occurred that could have led to such a fateful day? What kind of a man would be able to commit such a heartless crime? What drove him to view it as a rational and even necessary act? Was he truly a nut, or were his motivations understandable? If he bore such a twisted mind, how was he even able to function in an otherwise normal society? And how did the opportunity arise in the first place?

PROFILE OF A KILLER

One important contributing factor to Lee Harvey Oswald's actions was his violent nature. This aspect of his personality seems to have developed over a number of years. Evidence suggests that Oswald was peaceful and passive most of the time when he was a child. As a teenager, he became more likely to get into fights with other boys than simply walk away from a conflict. When he enlisted in the Marines at the age of 17, he was not only encouraged to perform violent acts, but also given the skills to become proficient in them.

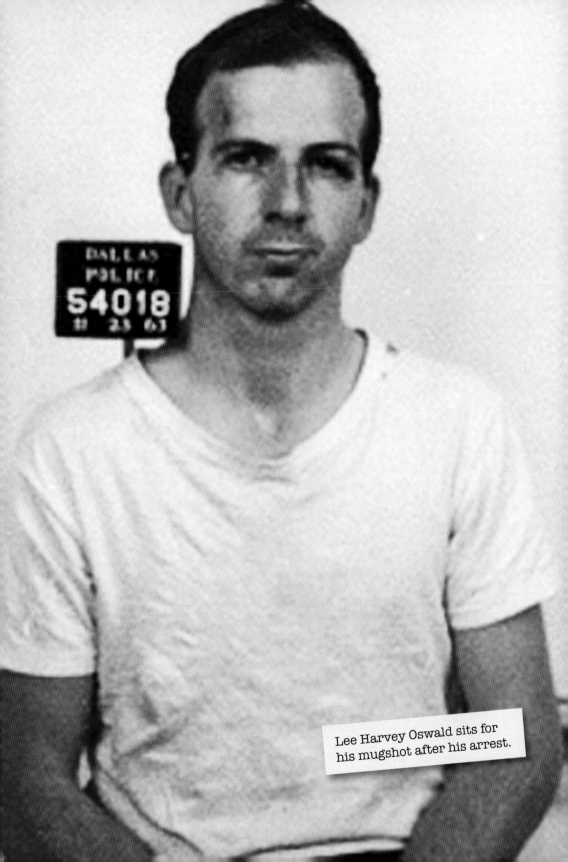

Lee Harvey Oswald sits for his mugshot after his arrest.

His marksmanship is one good example. His shooting record in the Marines showed he had a very respectable talent and was possibly capable of carrying out an execution such as the one performed on President Kennedy. And it is no secret that his marriage to Marina was marred by occasional instances of physical abuse.

Another factor appears to be Oswald's antisocial personality disorder. One trait of this condition is a lack of concern for the welfare of others. Oswald had a long history of general disinterest in other people, making virtually no friends in adulthood and avoiding human interaction as much as possible. Even at the age of 13, he is reported to have said to his school psychologist, "I dislike

Young Oswald stands among his second grade class in Fort Worth, Texas, in 1947.

everybody."[1] His relationship with his mother and two brothers was uneven (his father died before he was born), and he made no attempt to develop any substantial connection with others.

Oswald also suffered from a condition commonly called a "delusion of grandeur." In simplest terms, this is the belief by a person that he is superior to most others and is destined for greatness, even if his abilities do not suggest the potential to achieve anything of this magnitude. When giving legal testimony following the assassination, Marina Oswald stated for the record, "From everything I know about my husband and the events that transpired, I can conclude that he wanted in any way, whether good or bad, to do something that would make him outstanding, that he would be known in history."[2] A Texas lawyer who had known Oswald said, "My general impression . . . was that he wanted to become famous or infamous. That seemed to be his whole life ambition."[3] Oswald kept a journal at one point in his life that he called his "historic diary," believing every word that flowed from his pen was on par with holy gospel. He also loved to read biographies of famous figures, particularly politicians, and would often comment that he felt a kinship with such people. He even went so far as to boast that he would one day become a prime minister.

In addition, Oswald held an eternally burning anger. He was deeply frustrated with his life, having piled up a long record of failure and disappointment over the years. His outsized ambitions were inarguably part of the reason for this. Setting goals that were

Training received while Oswald was a U.S. Marine helped make him an excellent marksman.

unreachable put him on the fast track to bitterness. But even in the more everyday facets of life, he had maddening struggles. In school, he had trouble earning good grades (in spite of having what many noted was an above-average intelligence). In appearance, he was small and slight, creating an image of weakness. His time in the Marine Corps came to an inglorious end when he asked for a discharge under the false pretense that he had to help care for his aging mother. His tense and stormy marriage to Marina could hardly be considered successful. And while he apparently held great affection for his two young daughters, his ability to provide for them was substandard. He rarely kept a job for more than a few months, each one ending either with his being fired or him stalking out after a disagreement with his superiors (by all accounts, he loathed authority figures).

Even in his free time, he found himself surrounded by an American society that he came to despise, a capitalist system with which he felt increasingly out of step. And when he left America and moved to the Soviet Union in October 1959, he quickly became disillusioned with his experiences there as well. By the time President Kennedy came to Dallas in November 1963, Oswald had a history of letdowns. This, combined with his fierce desire to write himself into the history books, may have been important in motivating Oswald to kill the president.

Oswald met his wife Marina while living in Minsk in the Soviet Union.

Two-year-old Oswald poses for a picture.

Oswald's troubled childhood also has to be considered. By all accounts, it was marred by loneliness, longing, and neglect. Due to the death of his father two months before his birth in 1939, Oswald's mother had to go to work to provide for him and his two older brothers. Over the next few years, he was mostly raised by relatives. For a time, he was even placed in an orphanage. His mother could not afford babysitters, and the day care option familiar to many parents today did not exist at the time. Leaving the boy with friends apparently was not possible, either, as Oswald's mother—like Lee himself later on—was not big on building friendships. This led her into a long period of financial difficulties, dead-end jobs, and seething bitterness that, in turn, made Lee feel as though he was a burden to her.

NOT YET TO THE POINT OF NO RETURN

Even after years of difficulty with his mother and getting in trouble in school, Oswald was not beyond the point where he could have become a "normal" person. Due to his misbehavior, he sometimes had to meet with counselors. As one of them noted after spending long hours with the young man, there was "a rather pleasant, appealing quality about this emotionally starved, affectionless youngster, which grows as one speaks to him."[4] A social worker described Lee's mother as a "defensive, rigid, self-involved person who had real difficulty in accepting and relating to people."[5] The social worker's final estimation of Lee was, "There are indications that he has suffered serious personality damage, but if he can receive help quickly, this might be repaired to some extent."[6] That help never came, however.

Гостиница „МЕТРОПОЛЬ"

г. Москва

I Lee Harvey Oswald do hereby request that my present citizenship in the United States of America, be revoked.

I have entered the Soviet Union for the express purpose of appling for citizenship in the Soviet Union, through the means of naturalization.

My request for citizenship is now pending before the Supreme Soviet of the U.S.S.R..

I take these steps for political reasons.

My request for the revoking of my American citizenship is made only after the longest and most serious considerations.

I affirm that my allegiance is to the Union of Soviet Socialist Republics.

Oswald renounced his U.S. citizenship in a handwritten letter.

Commission Exhibit No. 257

The final piece of Oswald's complex psychological puzzle was his intense interest in political issues. In particular, he believed strongly in the superiority of communism (the idea that government should own and control all aspects of an economy) over capitalism (the idea that individuals should own and control their economy). Oswald felt the American way of life was inherently corrupt and evil, with the wealthiest and most powerful people manipulating the system to their personal advantage at the expense of everyone else. In a communist society, Oswald felt, there was greater equality. This attitude drove him, in October 1959, to travel to the Soviet Union—the epicenter of communism at the time—in hopes of becoming a Soviet citizen. When his application for citizenship was rejected, he was crushed. However, he had no intention of going back to America without a fight. Shortly after he received word of the denial, he slit his wrists in his hotel room, hoping the severity of the gesture would force the Soviet authorities to keep him.

He was brought to a Soviet hospital for both treatment and psychiatric observation. Upon his release, he went to a U.S. embassy and renounced his American citizenship. In a note handed to an embassy official, he wrote, "I take these steps for political reasons. My request for the revoking of my American citizenship is made only after the longest and most serious considerations. I affirm that my allegiance is to the Union of the Soviet Socialist Republics."[7] If his willingness to give up his citizenship in America does not seem like powerful enough evidence of devotion to his political beliefs, consider what he wrote to his own brother, Robert, to emphasize his belief in communism: "In the event of war I would kill any American who put a uniform on in defense of the American government—any American."[8]

Oswald was eventually permitted to stay in the Soviet Union, which delighted him to no end. He was given an apartment, a monthly subsidy (a government-funded allowance), and a job as a metalworker in a factory that made radios and televisions. He

Oswald (center, glasses) poses for a photo with friends in Minsk, USSR.

became socially active, making friends perhaps for the first time in his life, and settled into the communist dream he had craved. It was also during this time that he met and married Marina. One would think he would have been the happiest man in the world. But it was not so. Within a year of his arrival in the USSR, he was having second thoughts, feeling that the communist leaders were just as corrupt and self-serving as those in America, and that life in the Soviet Union was drab and boring for the ordinary citizen. By early 1961, he was working to undo his renunciation of American citizenship, and in June of the following year, he returned to America. His peculiar story earned mild attention from the press, which he enjoyed tremendously.

While he may have been disappointed in Soviet life, his devotion to communism was unchanged. Setting the Soviet Union aside, he refocused this devotion toward Fidel Castro, the communist leader of the island nation of Cuba. One of the main features of the Kennedy administration was a tense relationship with Castro. There had been multiple attempts by the U.S. government, at Kennedy's direction, to remove Castro from power. Oswald seemed to grow more enraged at each news story that underscored Kennedy's efforts.

The greatest irony of all, perhaps, is that Oswald did not dislike Kennedy at all. Marina Oswald testified after the assassination that "he always spoke very complimentary about the president."[9] But when it came to making a decision between Kennedy and Castro, Oswald clearly knew where his loyalties lay.

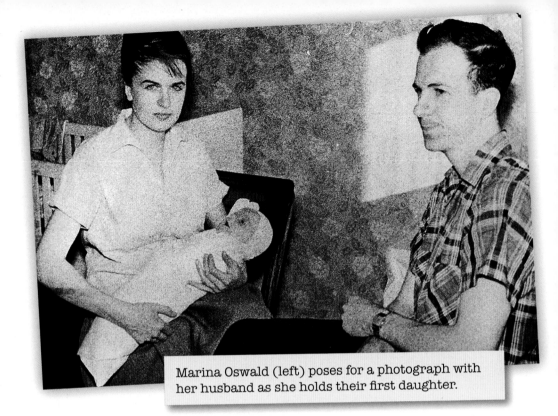

Marina Oswald (left) poses for a photograph with her husband as she holds their first daughter.

THE PEOPLE IN OSWALD'S LIFE

One argument made from time to time is that Oswald, while an isolated soul by nature, did not accomplish the assassination entirely on his own. There were those around him who, indirectly and without intent, enabled him to achieve his goal. One very likely candidate for this category was Oswald's wife. Marina knew him better than anyone and was allowed to see more of his otherwise carefully concealed personality. She knew of his violent tendencies, his craving for fame, and his hatred of the United States. She also knew of his fanatic devotion to Castro and the communist cause. She recounted a story from August 1963—just a few short months before the assassination—when she found him on the porch of their

THE NEAR-MURDER OF GENERAL EDWIN WALKER

In early October 1962, Oswald became upset by an article he read in the communist newspaper the *Daily Worker*. It focused on U.S. Major General Edwin A. Walker, a combat veteran of both World War II and the Korean War. Walker was known for his deeply conservative views, including a fierce belief that communism should be eradicated worldwide. In March 1963, he made a speech singling out Fidel Castro and his communist forces as a "scourge." A week later, Oswald mail-ordered the rifle he would later use to kill President Kennedy. He kept watch on Walker at his Dallas home for the next few weeks, then tried to shoot him through his dining room window on April 10. The bullet ricocheted off the wood in the window frame instead, leaving Walker unharmed. Police did not connect Oswald with the shooting until after he was arrested for the president's assassination. Oswald's wife, meanwhile, had known all about it. She hid the note he had written with instructions on what she should do in the event of his capture, and she watched him burn all written plans in their bathtub after the failed attack.

Major General Edwin Walker was Oswald's first attempt at assassination.

home, practice-aiming his rifle and saying, "Fidel Castro needs defenders. I'm going to join his army of volunteers. I'm going to be a revolutionary."[10] Perhaps most startling, though, was her knowledge of his attempt to murder General Edwin Walker seven months before he killed President Kennedy. Despite knowing about this crime, Marina never informed the authorities.

Both the CIA and FBI watched Oswald through the years, monitoring him in the Soviet Union and then more carefully when he came back. They knew he'd had Marine training, that he was a capable sharpshooter, and that he had extreme views about the United States and its government. However, they did not pick up on the clues that he was planning an attack.

ACQUISITION OF THE MURDER WEAPON

A truly thorough examination of the causes behind the Kennedy assassination has to include the ease with which Oswald acquired the murder weapon. The gun was a 6.5-millimeter Mannlicher-Carcano rifle with an inexpensive scope. Oswald used the name "A. Hidell" to purchase it through the mail from Klein's Sporting Goods, located in Chicago. The total cost for the rifle and scope including shipping, was just over $20. On top of that, he paid for it with a money order and had it delivered to a post office box that he had only recently opened (also under a false name). The entire transaction was suspicious, yet no one paused to take notice.

SELECTIVE SERVICE SYSTEM
NOTICE OF CLASSIFICATION · Approval not

ALEK _____ JAMES _____ HIDEL
(First name) (Middle name) (Last nam

Selective Service No. [42] [224] [39] [5521]
been classified in Class _____ I-W ___ (Until _____
19 _____) by ☐ Local Board ☐ Appea
by vote of _____ to _____ ☐ I
(Show vote on appeal board cases only)
_____, 19 _____ _____
(Date of mailing) (Member or clerk of local bo

The law requires you, subject to heavy penalty for violation, this notice, in addition to your Registration Certificate on you at all times—to exhibit it upon request to authorized officials render it to your commanding officer upon entering the armed f
The law requires you to notify your local board in writing (1) change in your address, physical condition, and occupational, family, dependency, and military status, and (2) of any other fa might change your classification.
FOR ADVICE, SEE YOUR GOVERNMENT APPEAL AC

Oswald used a fake draft card to purchase a rifle.

SECURITY ISSUES SURROUNDING THE PRESIDENT

It is no secret that President Kennedy requested the protective top on his limousine be removed the day he was assassinated. If it had been there, he might have survived. It may even be that, without the opportunity for a clear shot, Oswald would not have attempted the assassination. Kennedy had also requested that his Secret Service agents not stand on the running boards on either side of the car. If an agent had been that close, he would have been able to push the president down after, at the very least, the second bullet struck. In this sense, Kennedy helped Oswald by making himself unusually vulnerable.

Some of the blame must certainly lie with the Secret Service itself. The organization has a well-deserved reputation for the highest level of efficiency and competence. Yet none of its agents took notice of either Oswald or his rifle barrel sticking out of the sixth-floor window of the book depository. While there were thousands of people on the ground who all needed watching, there were also numerous tall buildings, with hundreds of windows and high rooftops—ideal positions from a sniper's perspective. Carefully scanning such areas is standard procedure for the Secret Service during a presidential visit. Several ordinary people spotted Oswald and his weapon, but somehow none of the agents did.

The president's cars had special footstands along the side for Secret Service agents.

CHAPTER THREE

THE DRAMA CONTINUES

★ ★ ★

President Kennedy died almost immediately after being shot on November 22, 1963. But in many ways, the shooting itself was only the beginning of the saga. As a grieving public struggled with the shock of the president's death, new events transpired that were so dramatic as to defy believability.

Newspapers across the country announced the president's death.

THE DAILY LIGHT Has 15,606 or 28.9% More Home Delivered

Third Extra

THE
SAN ANTONIO TEXAS

Telephone CA6-2441

83rd YEAR—NO. 307 ★★★★★ FRIDAY, NOVEMBER 22, 1963   52 PAGES 5 CENTS

Classified CA6-2331

JFK SHOT TO DEATH!
CONNALLY WOUNDED

Hidden Assassin Used Rifle

DALLAS (AP)--President John F. Kennedy, 36th President of the United States, was shot to death today by a hidden assassin armed with a high-powered rifle.

Kennedy, 46, lived less than an hour after a sniper cut him down as his limousine left downtown Dallas.

Connally Denies 'Real' Rift

Jack Ruby (center) was among the crowd at the Dallas police station on November 22, after President Kennedy's assassination.

A MAN NAMED RUBY

Following the assassination, schools and businesses were closed, flags were flown at half-staff, and religious services were held. Even Kennedy's biggest critics were taken by a sense of loss and regret. One Texas man who had voted for Richard Nixon, Kennedy's opponent in the 1960 presidential election, said, "I wanted him out of office, but not this way."[1]

As for Kennedy's supporters and admirers, most were struck with feelings of confusion, despair, and, in some cases, rage. One example of the latter was a Dallas businessman named Jack Ruby.

AMERICAN PRIDE

Although owning a seedy nightclub was not exactly considered a reputable profession, Ruby took great pride in the fact that he lived in a nation where a poor kid from the streets of Chicago could become a business owner at all. Ruby believed in the popular notion that America was the land of opportunity, and he was fiercely proud to be one of the country's citizens. If he heard nightclub customers talk negatively about the country, he would throw them out. He also refused to allow comedians performing at the club to make jokes about America or its government. When Ruby went to baseball games, he was known to scold people for not removing their hats, putting out their cigarettes, or taking a break from eating as the national anthem played. He even got into fistfights from time to time over his intense love for the nation.

Born in Chicago on March 25, 1911, Ruby began working for the Mafia while he was still a teenager. He then moved to Dallas to manage a nightclub. He opened his own club, which he called the Carousel, in the mid-1950s.

Ruby was a huge fan of Kennedy, and news of the assassination hit him hard. He closed down his nightclub as a show of respect and was angered when other club owners in Dallas didn't do the same. He called friends, relatives, and employees to talk about the tragedy, rambling incoherently between sobs. By the end of the day, he had become physically ill and was unable to sleep or eat. He felt a growing fury at the man responsible for taking the president's life.

Ruby went to the Dallas police station late that night. He was friends with many of the officers on the force. Some of them visited the Carousel occasionally, and Ruby always made sure they were "taken care of" with free drinks, food, and so on. He also helped the police by passing along information about crimes that he overheard people talking about in his club. In return for his ongoing help, the police allowed Ruby to roam about freely in their midst.

Standing in the station hallway around midnight, Ruby knew that Oswald had already been captured, arrested, and interrogated. He waited with dozens of journalists for Oswald to be moved from the police chief's office to a tiny holding cell. When Oswald finally appeared amid a hail of questions, he walked within a few feet of Ruby, who studied him carefully.

President Kennedy's casket was displayed in the East Room of the White House.

NOVEMBER 23

In the early hours of the morning, at a naval hospital in Bethesda, Maryland, undertakers went through the grim task of preparing President Kennedy's body for burial. It was not easy, considering the damage that had been done. Finally, Kennedy's body was transported to Washington, D.C. around 4:00 a.m. Jackie and the president's brother, Robert, decided that the coffin should remain closed during the funeral. The coffin was brought to the East Room of the White House, and shortly after 10:00 a.m., there was a private service for members of the Kennedy family and their close friends. Then the service became public as the image of Kennedy's flag-covered coffin was broadcast over live television throughout the country and around the world.

Around this time, Lee Harvey Oswald was being interrogated again. He took on a smug, arrogant demeanor, flatly denying some statements he had made earlier, while refusing to talk altogether at other times. When he found himself cornered, he would often reply with, "I don't have to answer that" or "Not without the advice of my [legal] counsel."[2] He became particularly agitated whenever he was presented with hard evidence, such as when the police presented him with an identification card that had his picture and handwriting on it but a false name he had obviously invented. The Dallas police had already formally charged him with the murders of both Kennedy and Tippit at this point, as there was more than enough evidence against him. However, they were hoping to get more information out of him, maybe even a confession.

Shortly after 1:00 p.m., Oswald was visited by his wife and his mother. He was happy to see the former but not the latter. He said to Marina in Russian, "Why did you bring that fool with you? I don't want to see her."[3] Marina tried to calm him down. Her main concern, though, was trying to get a feel for whether her husband was really guilty of such a terrible crime. It didn't take long for her to decide that he was. If he had been wrongly arrested and accused, he would've been wild with anger. But she thought that he seemed quiet, resigned, and even a little bit frightened—emotions that were uncommon for him. When Oswald finally had to leave the room and return to his cell, Marina began crying.

Oswald talks to reporters as officials escort him through the Dallas police station.

Marina Oswald visited her husband with their second daughter and Lee's mother.

Jack Ruby woke up late in the day in a bad mood that quickly worsened. Around 3:00 p.m., he went to Dealey Plaza. When he saw all the other grief-stricken visitors and the flowers that had been left in Kennedy's honor, he broke down again. Eventually he went to his sister's apartment, where he finally fell asleep, physically and emotionally exhausted.

Meanwhile, Dallas police searched the home where Marina and the Oswalds' two children were staying. The police had been there once before, but this time they wanted to go through some bags and boxes in the garage. They eventually came upon two black-

Oswald poses in his backyard with the Mannlicher-Carcano rifle that he would use to shoot the president.

and-white photographs of Oswald holding the same kind of rifle that was used to shoot the president. In the photos, he also wore a handgun in a hip holster—the same type of gun used to kill Officer Tippit. The officers then discovered materials Oswald had used to make one of his false identification cards.

Back at the police station, around 6:30 p.m., Oswald was presented with this powerful evidence. To no one's surprise, he claimed the photographs were fakes created as part of an effort to frame him. He also claimed that he had never seen the false ID material before, in spite of the fact that a handwriting expert had already claimed the penmanship was a perfect match to his. Oswald then stated once again that he would not cooperate any further without his lawyer present. However, no one had been able to locate the lawyer Oswald was requesting. It was not long after this interrogation that the Dallas police decided they could do no more with Oswald. It was time to move him out of their building and into the nearby county jail to await trial for the two murders—a trial that some were already predicting would be the "greatest of the 20th century." They would move him the next day, they decided.

NOVEMBER 24

Jack Ruby woke up feeling no better two days after the assassination. He finally snapped when he saw two items in the morning newspaper. One was a letter written by the father of two young girls to President Kennedy's five-year-old daughter, Caroline. The father and his children had come out to see the president on November 22, and Kennedy had made a point of smiling and waving to them. "I thought your daddy must love little boys and little girls very much," the father wrote. "Only one who understands and loves little children would realize just how much it would mean to them to be noticed in the presence of so many adults. I thought then how much he must love you."[4]

A SON'S MOVING TRIBUTE

President Kennedy's memorial took place over the three days following his assassination, from November 23 to November 25. On the first day, his coffin lay in the East Room of the White House. On the second day, it was moved to the Capitol to lie in state. Hundreds of thousands of mourners came to pay their respects, including former presidents Eisenhower and Truman, countless other American politicians, and nearly 100 heads of foreign nations. Just before 11:00 a.m. on the third day, the coffin was brought by horse-drawn caisson (a two-wheeled wagon) to St. Matthew's Cathedral, where Kennedy and his family had often attended mass. More than 1,000 guests attended the service. Afterward, the coffin was readied for its final journey to Arlington National Cemetery. Just after it was brought out of the cathedral, John F. Kennedy Jr., the president's three-year-old son, stepped forward and raised his little hand in a military salute to honor his late father. This became one of the most memorable images of the 20th century.

Then he saw something else—an article stating that Oswald's trial might require Jackie to return to Dallas and testify as an eyewitness. That meant she would have to relive the entire horrid experience. The very thought of this drove Ruby to near madness. He could not bear the thought of Jackie having to endure such torment. Around 11:00 a.m., he left his sister's home and returned to his own apartment, where he slipped a revolver into his pocket and left again, heading for the Dallas police station.

About this time, the police were getting ready to transfer Oswald to the county jail. They were on the third floor, and the plan was to take him to the basement and into an unmarked police car. Around 11:20 a.m., Oswald was handcuffed to an officer named Jim Leavelle. Leavelle and Oswald were surrounded by other police. They all began walking toward the elevator. Leavelle said jokingly to Oswald, "Lee, if anybody shoots at you, I hope they're as good a shot as you are." Oswald's response was, "Aw, there ain't going to be anybody shooting at me."[5]

LIVE ON TELEVISION

Ruby was outside the station at this point, standing on the sidewalk by the vehicle ramp that led to the basement. An officer was posted there to make sure no one went down the ramp. Ruby knew this officer well, and when he saw Ruby he thought nothing of it. Ruby waited until the officer was distracted, then went down the ramp. At the bottom, he found a tense, chaotic scene. There were reporters and photographers everywhere. They all knew Oswald was coming.

Jack Ruby shot and killed Oswald while millions watched the incident live on national television.

The reporters had their pencils ready, preparing to shout questions at Oswald even though the police told them not to. Others had cameras, both for still photos and live video feeds.

The elevator doors opened at the end of the hallway, and Oswald appeared with officers around him. As the group began moving through the crowd, the questions came fast and furious. Oswald ignored them all. Every camera lens was pointed in his direction. He had no expression on his face—just like during the interrogations, he gave nothing away. When he came within a few feet of Jack Ruby, Ruby reached into his pocket, took out his revolver, and stepped forward. Before anyone knew what was happening, he fired one shot low into Oswald's chest. Oswald doubled over with a groan and fell to the floor.

All of this occurred on live television, where millions of Americans witnessed the first-ever publicly broadcast murder. A few officers jumped on Ruby and wrestled the gun away, while others called for an ambulance and tended to Oswald. One officer, seeing that Oswald was still conscious, asked him if he had anything to say. Oswald shook his head no. Then he faded out of consciousness and was taken to Parkland Memorial Hospital, the same place where the president had been treated three days earlier. Oswald's condition quickly worsened due to massive blood loss, and he was pronounced dead just after 1:00 p.m.

Officials place Oswald on a stretcher to transfer him from the police station to the hospital.

CHAPTER FOUR

THE ULTIMATE WHODUNIT

★ ★ ★

Even after the death of Lee Harvey Oswald, America was far from ready to close the case on the assassination. Too many questions remained unanswered, and the assassination would inspire discussion and debate for years to come. Often, investigation into one of the case's many mysteries only served to spawn several more.

Police officers found Oswald's rifle, bullets, identification, and other items while investigating Kennedy's assassination.

Ruby answers a reporter's questions as police officers move him to a jail cell.

THE FATE OF JACK RUBY

Immediately after shooting Lee Harvey Oswald, Jack Ruby was taken into custody by Dallas police and charged with murder. On March 14, 1964, he was convicted and sentenced to death. Shortly thereafter, however, one of Ruby's lawyers filed an appeal claiming that the sentence had been unfair because the trial should not have been held in Dallas. The appeals court that reviewed the complaint agreed and ordered that Ruby's sentence be overturned and a new trial held. This new trial never occurred, though. In late 1966, Ruby was admitted to Parkland Memorial Hospital to be treated for pneumonia. There, it was discovered that he had advanced cancer throughout his body. Ruby died on January 3, 1967.

The Warren Commission included several members of Congress, as well as Chief Justice Earl Warren (center) and future president Gerald Ford (far left).

THE WARREN COMMISSION

In spite of the overwhelming evidence against Lee Harvey Oswald, Lyndon Johnson knew a full investigation of the Kennedy assassination would be necessary to satisfy the government and the American people. To this end, he ordered the formation of the President's Commission on the Assassination of President Kennedy on November 29, 1963. Its seven-member team was led by Earl Warren, then chief justice of the Supreme Court, and thus became more commonly known as the Warren Commission. (Another notable member was Gerald R. Ford, then a U.S. representative from Michigan, who would later become the 38th president of the United States.) Johnson asked the Warren Commission to oversee an exhaustive, impartial investigation into the assassination and provide a full report.

Over the next 10 months, the commission and its many aides visited numerous locations, examined key pieces of evidence, and took testimony from hundreds of people. Their final conclusions, issued to President Johnson in September 1964, were that Lee Harvey Oswald was the only person involved in the assassination, that he was driven by political radicalism as well as a variety of mental illnesses, and that he fired three bullets—the first missing its intended target, the second wounding both Kennedy and Connally, and the third causing the president's fatal wound to the head.

The commission's findings became known as the "lone-gunman theory." However, there were many questions about the event that the commission's report did not answer. Many skeptics were convinced the killing was the result of a conspiracy. From this belief came a movement to "uncover the truth" about the assassination. Their mission, then, was to find out who was really behind the plan to kill Kennedy and what actually happened in Dealey Plaza that day. The resulting theories have ranged from barely plausible to outright crazy, but they live on. Today, more than two-thirds of the American public continue to believe that Lee Harvey Oswald did not act alone.

A FEW CONSPIRACY THEORIES

Among the many conspiracy theories, one of the most popular is that there was a second gunman in Dealey Plaza—that Oswald was not the only person who fired on the president. Of the roughly 100 eyewitnesses who were there that day, nearly one-third claimed that the shots came from somewhere in front of the president rather than behind him. Some of these people believed that the gunman in question was positioned behind a fence at the top of a small, grass-covered hill that became famously known as the "grassy knoll." Supporting this claim was evidence that

1. the president's head pitched back when the third and fatal bullet hit, indicating that the shot must have come from in front of him;

2. it would have been impossible for Oswald to fire three accurate shots in eight seconds with the rifle he used; and

3. the witnesses heard these shots in front of the president, but did not see anyone.

Concerning who actually arranged the assassination, theories vary. One is that the Central Intelligence Agency (CIA) was behind it. The reasoning includes the theory that Kennedy may have wanted to

Many people believe another shooter stood on the "grassy knoll" (left), not far from the Texas School Book Depository.

eliminate the CIA following its disastrous attempt to overthrow Castro's Cuban government in what became known as the Bay of Pigs invasion. The CIA formulated the invasion and hired and trained the soldiers who participated. Their attempts were crushed by Cuban forces, and the failure cast the Kennedy administration in an embarrassing light. In response, Kennedy told one of his advisers, "I want to splinter the CIA into a thousand pieces and scatter them to the four winds."[1] To keep their agency intact and to cover up other illegal activities, CIA leaders were believed by some conspiracy theorists to have plotted to eliminate Kennedy before he had a chance to do any damage. Having expert assassins at their disposal and being able to manipulate records

The Cuban military captured more than 1,000 of the CIA-trained soldiers who participated in the Bay of Pigs invasion.

Like other CIA targets, Fidel Castro was a powerful political leader who was considered a threat to the United States.

and get access to key information such as the president's schedule and motorcade route on November 22, the CIA therefore should have been able to pull off the assassination with relative ease. It is interesting to note that the CIA was, in fact, the target of a formal investigation in the mid-1970s concerning plots to assassinate leaders of foreign governments, including Fidel Castro, Patrice Lumumba of the Democratic Republic of the Congo, and Ngo Dinh Diem of Vietnam.

Similar to the CIA theory is the idea that the Federal Bureau of Investigation (FBI) was behind the killing. At the time of the shooting, the FBI was under the direction of J. Edgar Hoover. Hoover began working for the bureau during World War I and spent his entire career there. He had developed the sinister habit

FBI director J. Edgar Hoover (center) meets with
President John Kennedy (left) and Robert Kennedy.

of investigating the personal lives of high-ranking politicians
in hopes of finding the kind of "dirt" that could be used as
blackmail material. This was his way of gaining power over the
country's leaders. With President Kennedy, who'd had numerous
extramarital affairs, Hoover had plenty to work with. But he did
not have the same kind of success putting a leash on Kennedy's
brother, Robert, who, as attorney general, was Hoover's superior.
Hoover and Robert Kennedy had a stormy relationship based on
mutual dislike, and Hoover likely felt threatened by him. Hoover
also worried that President Kennedy would force him to retire from
his beloved post, which Kennedy would have had the power to do.
With these factors in play, some conspiracy experts believe, Hoover
had reason to seek Kennedy's elimination.

The organized crime group known popularly as the Mafia has
also long been suspected of carrying out the assassination. Their

motive, it is thought, was that Kennedy's brother, Robert, began an unprecedented effort to wipe out their American operations after he became attorney general. Killing the president, the theory goes, would prevent Robert Kennedy from continuing his crusade. As with the CIA and the FBI, the Mafia certainly had its share of trained killers. Furthermore, there is strong evidence to suggest a connection between the Mafia and the Kennedy family. Joe Kennedy, the president's father, had sought assistance from the Mafia to help his son win the 1960 presidential election. Mobsters in Illinois cast hundreds, if not thousands, of illegal votes so that Kennedy would win the state, which turned out to be crucial in one of the closest elections in American history. When Kennedy reached the White House as a result of this assistance, the Mafia expected him to, at the very least, take a passive, "turn-the-other-cheek" stance toward their illegal activities. Many conspiracy theorists believe, therefore, that Robert Kennedy's crusade to cripple the Mafia in America directly resulted in his brother's death.

Several conspiracy buffs have suggested that Vice President Johnson was the mastermind behind the assassination. This is almost believable if one considers that Johnson had the most to gain: upon Kennedy's death, he would automatically become the new president. And this, it has been suggested, was just one of his motivations. Another was the fact that Johnson had a tense relationship with both the president and his brother, Robert, and that the Kennedys were planning to replace him as vice president for the 1964 election. There is further suggestion that Johnson was aided by a small group of Texas oil barons, who helped fund the assassination in return for Johnson's favoritism once he assumed the presidency. The notion that Johnson was directly involved in the assassination has also been supported by a handful of people who knew him well, including a former mistress and a CIA agent.

One theory that has stood the test of time is that the assassination was the handiwork of Fidel Castro. Some years after Kennedy's assassination, it was revealed that the CIA had led a secret plot to kill Castro in the early 1960s that ultimately failed—and that Robert Kennedy, and perhaps President Kennedy as well, had known all about it. With this in mind, it is not difficult to believe that Castro would have wanted to eliminate the president in retaliation. In October 1968, Lyndon Johnson told a journalist that he believed "Kennedy was trying to get to Castro, but Castro got to him first."[2] The fact that Oswald was a devoted fan of Castro made this idea all the more plausible, as Oswald would likely have been honored to carry out such a task for someone he so deeply admired.

A similar theory to the Castro plot is that leaders of the Soviet Union were behind the assassination. The motivation in this instance is supposedly that the Soviets had been deeply humiliated by the Cuban Missile Crisis. This was a showdown between the United States and both the Soviet Union and Cuba after it was discovered that the Soviets were building bases in Cuba from which missiles could easily strike key U.S. targets such as New York City

A U.S. naval ship (bottom) near Cuba runs alongside a Soviet cargo ship for an inspection.

and Washington, D.C. Tensions reached such a high point between America and the Soviets—by far the two greatest superpowers in the world at the time—that many experts now believe it was the closest humanity ever came to an all-out nuclear war. President Kennedy eventually ordered a naval quarantine around Cuba, essentially using naval ships to stop the shipment of missiles, and demanded that the Soviets remove all existing missiles and dismantle their bases in Cuba. They did, and this made the Soviets look weak and humiliated in comparison to America, leading some to believe that a handful of Soviet leaders eventually arranged Kennedy's assassination as a form of revenge.

It is also important to note that various conspiracy theorists

OTHER THEORIES

Some of the lesser-known theories about the assassination range from bizarre to outright silly. They should still be mentioned, however, since conspiracy enthusiasts have taken the time to write books and articles about them, making them part of the public imagination. One theory holds that Kennedy was killed by high-ranking members of the financial industry out of fear that he was planning to eliminate the Federal Reserve System. Another claims that the Secret Service was behind the killing, knowing that an assassin was waiting and making the choice to leave the president exposed. A third offers the idea that the government of Israel played a role in the assassination due to the pressure Kennedy was putting on them to be more forthcoming about their pursuit of nuclear weapons.

One particularly absurd theory states that General Walker arranged the assassination in order to frame Oswald for the attempt on his life some months earlier. There have also been claims that Oswald had a body double who acted as a decoy so he could escape Dallas; that Jack Ruby was sent by the Kennedy family via their Mafia connections to kill Oswald in revenge of his killing the president; that the president's body had been tampered with by Secret Service agents to cover up his actual wounds; and—perhaps most ridiculous of all—that Kennedy actually survived the shooting and, in a severely handicapped state, lived out the rest of his life on a tiny island in the Mediterranean.

have claimed any combination of the above—that the FBI worked together with the Mafia to carry out the assassination, or that Castro's people worked with the CIA, etc. What makes some of these assertions difficult to believe is the simple fact that the more people involved in such a plot, the less likely that it could be kept a secret for so many years. It should also be noted that all of the above theories have suffered from a lack of hard evidence, making them impossible to prove.

THE HOUSE SELECT COMMITTEE ON ASSASSINATIONS

Many people continue to feel strongly that a conspiracy was behind President Kennedy's assassination.

In 1976, a government committee was formed to investigate the controversial shootings of three notable figures: Alabama governor George Wallace, civil rights leader Dr. Martin Luther King Jr., and President Kennedy. It became known as the United States House of Representatives Select Committee on Assassinations, abbreviated to the House Select Committee on Assassinations (HSCA). The committee was involved because of growing public pressure from the belief that the Warren Commission's findings were flawed in light of new evidence and testimony that had surfaced since the original investigation.

Most who believed Oswald acted alone and felt the HSCA would arrive at the same conclusion were stunned when the committee's 1979 report stated that the president's death was, in fact, likely

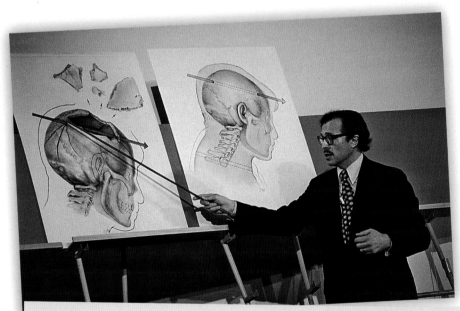

New York chief medical examiner Michael Baden discusses Kennedy's head wounds before the House Assassination Committee.

the result of a conspiracy. The HSCA's central evidence for this conclusion was based on a sound recording taken from a radio transmitter on one of the Dallas police motorcycles that had been accidentally stuck in the "on" position. The recording suggested that four shots, not three, had been fired. This, the committee decided, was proof of a second shooter, as it would have been impossible for Oswald to make four shots in eight seconds. However, the HSCA failed to provide evidence as to what organization had hired this other shooter, what that organization's motives were, and so on. Furthermore, the HSCA stated that it had found no proof of involvement in the assassination by any American government agency (such as the CIA or FBI), foreign government (Cuba or the Soviet Union), or crime organization (the Mafia).

Since the release of the HSCA report, several problems have been found with its stuck-transmitter theory. One is that there is evidence that the recording with the supposed shots was made a short time after the assassination took place, suggesting that the sounds heard on it were not gunshots at all. Also, the officer who was on the motorcycle bearing the transmitter was not believed to be near the president's limousine at the precise time of the shooting. Finally, exhaustive examination of all photos and film taken in Dealey Plaza at the time of the assassination suggest that there were no police motorcycles in the area where the recordings supposedly took place.

A CHANGE OF HEART

Among the most convincing evidence against Oswald was the simple fact that his wife, Marina, testified that she believed he was guilty when she was interviewed by the Warren Commission. Her precise words were, "I have no doubt that he did kill the president." When asked specifically about his motives, she told the commission, "I came to the conclusion that he wanted in any way, by any means, good or bad, to get into history. . . . I think there was some political foundation to it, a foundation of which I am not aware."[3] The Warren Commission gave tremendous credibility to her testimony, as Marina likely knew her husband better than anyone.

And yet, many years later, she made a complete turnaround on the issue. In 1996, she was interviewed by talk show host Oprah Winfrey. When Winfrey asked Marina if she still believed her husband had anything to do with the assassination, she replied in her Russian-tinged English, "Absolutely nothing." She further said, "[I]t's not an overnight conclusion, and it's not because I read books, and this book and that book." When Winfrey reminded Marina of her Warren Commission testimony, she said, "Absolutely. And the Warren Commission came to the conclusion and this question was asked after all the testimonies were done: 'Mrs. Oswald, now with the evidence in front of you, what do you know, what is your conclusion? Was your husband innocent or guilty?' You cannot know because some evidence was there and in the middle of the table was a rifle, which I identified as Lee's rifle, and I was a stupid young girl and right now if you show me my

Decades after the assassination, Marina Oswald Porter came to believe that Lee Harvey Oswald was not guilty.

husband's hunting rifle and I would be smart enough to say that I am not sure because up to this date I know nothing about this rifle. I'm not saying it was Lee's or not, but I trusted so blindly that it must be his rifle."[4]

When Marina was further interviewed by famed attorney and author Vincent Bugliosi in late 2000, she told him, "Lee was set up as a patsy." When Bugliosi asked who was responsible, she cited the CIA, the FBI, Lyndon Johnson, the Mafia, and Castro, among others. When Bugliosi made the point that that was a lot of different people and different organizations, her response was that "they all work together." Bugliosi felt as though Marina had been affected by all the conspiracy theories put forth over the years, but she hinted that she had information no one else knew about, saying, "There are certain things only for me to know."[5]

CHAPTER FIVE

ECHOES

★ ★ ★

In spite of the fact that the Kennedy assassination occurred more than half a century ago, the proverbial echoes of the three shots fired that day can still be heard. In a poll conducted by ABC News in 2003 in observation of the assassination's 40th anniversary, 70 percent of those surveyed believed the president was the victim of a conspiracy. Only 22 percent believed Oswald acted alone, with the remaining 8 percent uncertain. This was up sharply from a 1966 poll where only 46 percent felt a conspiracy occurred.

Actor Kevin Costner uses a model of Dealey Plaza to explain a theory on Kennedy's assassination in the film *JFK*.

RENEWED PUBLIC OUTRAGE

The 1991 film *JFK*, directed by Oliver Stone, did much to fan the flames of public suspicion. Based on conspiracy theories, and with some parts shot in a documentary-like style, the film supported the notion that countless government agencies and high officials were in on the assassination, including members of the CIA, the FBI, the military, and the Mafia, as well as Lyndon Johnson. The film was also loosely based on the real-life efforts of New Orleans district attorney Jim Garrison to uncover all guilty parties and secure the first prosecutions in the assassination. In actuality, Garrison managed just one prosecution during his famous crusade, that of New Orleans businessman Clay Shaw, but Shaw was eventually acquitted. The movie was nominated for eight Academy Awards, won two, and undoubtedly converted millions of Americans into firm believers that Kennedy's death was plotted by more than one frustrated individual searching for glory.

Another disturbing phenomenon that has continued to stir the pot of public paranoia is the number of people related to the assassination who died under unusual or mysterious circumstances in the years immediately following. In 1964 alone, more than a dozen such people passed away unexpectedly. One, a CIA operative who claimed the agency had taken part in the assassination, was found dead with a gunshot to the head. It was ruled a suicide. A woman who had been heard trying to warn people of the assassination before it occurred was murdered. A different woman who also claimed to have advance knowledge of the assassination was killed in a hit-and-run accident, with those responsible for her death never found. Two witnesses who were prepared to testify in court that they knew of a connection between the Mafia and some of the CIA's political assassination plots were both killed before they could speak. Were these and many other deaths directly related to the assassination? It is impossible to say, but it certainly had a chilling effect on the American people.

The movie *JFK* did have one substantial positive effect concerning the assassination: it drove the public to demand that the federal government open up all official records pertaining to the assassination. Prior to the movie's release, most of this material had been kept secret. Then, in 1992, Congress passed the President John F. Kennedy Assassination Records Collection Act, which called for the collection and public release of all materials relating to the assassination. In October of that year, president George H. W. Bush signed the act into law. His successor, Bill Clinton, put together a five-member review board to collect these records—which, due to the sheer volume involved, took a number of years. This board also had to determine if any records should remain secret in order to protect innocent persons still alive.

A very small percentage of material remains unavailable. The remaining majority, however—more than five million documents, photographs, films, sound recordings, and miscellaneous artifacts—have been declassified and are, to this day, available for public

President Bill Clinton meets with the Assassination Records Review Board in 1998.

scrutiny. And while most people applauded this as a shining example of life in a free society, staunch conspiracy enthusiasts found little that deviated from the Warren Commission's lone-gunman theory—causing some of them to believe even more firmly that the real evidence is still locked away deep in some government vault. Whether this is true or not may be revealed in 2017, the year that all remaining records are due to be released.

SILVER LININGS

A handful of other societal improvements followed the assassination. First, there were some long-overdue advancements in gun control. When word spread of the ease with which Oswald had acquired the murder weapon, politicians in Washington set to work writing legislation that would enact stricter ownership requirements for guns. When civil rights leader Martin Luther King Jr. was shot to death in April 1968, followed by the killing of Robert Kennedy in June, this legislation began moving with a greater sense of urgency. President Johnson signed the Gun Control Act of 1968 into law on October 22. Among its many provisions was the denial of gun ownership to anyone who had been convicted of

The murder of Martin Luther King Jr. and other assassinations helped spark laws controlling gun ownership.

Over the decades, federal and state lawmakers have enacted a number of laws regulating gun ownership and use.

a serious crime, was considered a fugitive from justice, used illegal substances, was in the country illegally, had been dishonorably discharged from the armed forces, had been judged unstable by a mental institution, or was under the age of 18. It also severely limited the sales of firearms from one state to another—something that would have hampered Oswald's efforts, as he had received his rifle from a dealer in Illinois while living in Texas.

There were also many improvements made to the Secret Service's presidential security efforts. Congress, which determined the organization's budget, was more than happy to increase the amount of money it received. This, in turn, permitted the organization to hire more agents and make other operational improvements. The limousine in which Kennedy was shot, for example, underwent radical changes. After being examined during

The design of the presidential limousine has undergone significant changes since 1963.

the investigation and then thoroughly cleaned, it was rebuilt with a focus on protection rather than appearance. Armor plating was applied in numerous areas, including the underside in case someone tried to throw an explosive device beneath it. An armored top was permanently affixed, and ordinary glass replaced with the bulletproof variety. A high-performance engine was added for greater speed and power, as well as the best available transmission, brakes, suspension, and tires. The president is no longer allowed to ride in an open vehicle, having to instead satisfy himself with waving to passersby from within a cocoon of armored steel and bulletproof glass.

The Secret Service also expanded its efforts to investigate all people who might pose a threat to the president while traveling outside Washington. The Warren Commission criticized the Secret Service's lack of communication with agencies such as the CIA, the FBI, and the Departments of State and Defense, as well as local law enforcement. Any one of these could have provided information about Oswald that would have raised a red flag. After the assassination, the Secret Service became much more aggressive about gathering such intelligence during trip preparations, and its lists of suspicious individuals quickly increased from a few hundred to several thousand. Such suspects include those known to belong to anti-American organizations, those who had been dishonorably discharged from the armed forces, or those who had a history of violence.

A Secret Service agent greets local law enforcement during a presidential visit to Chicago, Illinois.

PROTECTING A PRESIDENT

An example of the value of the Secret Service's improved security in the years following the Kennedy assassination was described in a 1967 issue of Popular Science. President Johnson was giving a speech in New York City in February 1966. "When Mr. Johnson was interrupted by a man who climbed on a chair and shouted 'Peace in Vietnam,' the heckler was hustled away by two tablemates. It was no coincidence that the two tablemates were Secret Service agents. The Service had received the 1500-name guest list at four that afternoon. A quick check with the New York City police Special Squad brought word that the man was a potential troublemaker." Whether or not the heckler in question would have posed a threat to President Johnson's health is a matter of speculation, for the man was not carrying a weapon of any kind. But through the Secret Service's preventive practice of checking out people who might come in close contact with a visiting president, many incidents—ranging from embarrassing to deadly—have no doubt been avoided.[1]

Two Secret Service agents keep watch from a rooftop as the president has dinner across the street.

Another practice that the Secret Service improved was the examination of areas in which the president would be traveling. Sensitive to the criticism concerning Kennedy's exposure to so many tall buildings with high roofs and open windows in Dallas on the day of the assassination, the Service now thoroughly evaluates all such high-risk zones long before the president arrives. It has the power to close entire floors of buildings, lock doors and windows, seal off streets, and more. It also uses disguised agents to watch for suspicious activity in the days and weeks leading up to a presidential arrival. An example of this was noted by a former Amtrak employee in northern New Jersey in 1986: "I was working in one of the ticket booths in Penn Station at the time, and President Reagan was due to arrive in about two weeks. Since

I worked the night shift, I was familiar with a lot of the vagrants who hung around the station during the night hours. About a week before the president's arrival, I noticed a few new people hanging around the station—people I'd never seen before. They looked like any of the other drunks and wanderers, with grubby clothes and bottles of liquor wrapped in brown paper. But they seemed more alert than the others, more watchful. After Reagan's visit, they all disappeared. I never saw them again."[2]

EFFECT ON THE AMERICAN PSYCHE

The assassination of President Kennedy left a permanent scar on the psyche of the American public. Many still claim it was the end of America's "golden age" following World War II, a period characterized by unprecedented economic growth, unlimited hope for the future, and a certain childlike innocence. The latter seemed to be particularly compromised due to the brutal nature of the killing, followed by that of Oswald on live television two days later. When rumors of a possible conspiracy began and the government seemed unwilling to come clean with what it knew, a period of mistrust in American leadership began as well. There had always been some who were skeptical of those in power, but they were not as numerous and their cynicism was less intense. In the years following the assassination, people began to doubt those in power like never before. They became fearful of their own government and began wondering who was really safe if the president could be gunned down in cold blood. This disillusionment grew as the years

Thousands of people visit President Kennedy's grave each year.

passed without any clear answers. Then came the deceptions of the Vietnam War, followed by Richard Nixon's Watergate scandal, Ronald Reagan's Iran-Contra Affair . . . and on and on.

To this day, a lack of trust in government authority is widespread in America. What began on November 22, 1963, has in many ways never disappeared. More than the president's life was taken away. Stolen too was some crucial element that had been responsible for making the United States one of the greatest nations on the planet. John F. Kennedy knew of that greatness, and it is unlikely that a man of such faith and vision would have wanted the American people to become so consumed by the ugliness that took

American involvement in the Vietnam War, which lasted from 1954 to 1975, was highly controversial.

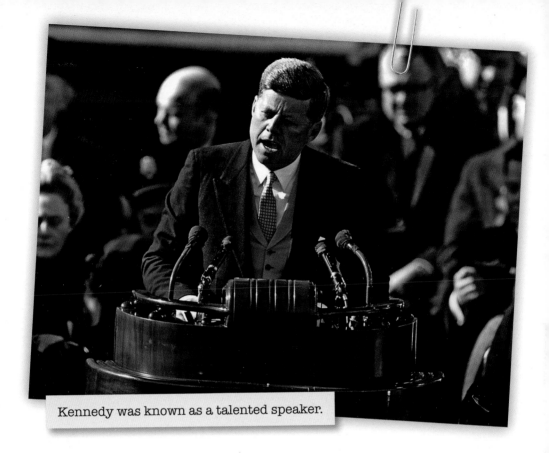

Kennedy was known as a talented speaker.

him from us. Perhaps the words he left unspoken in the speech he
was due to give that afternoon provide the inspiration to overcome
the trauma of those dark hours:

"We ask . . . that we may be worthy of our power and
responsibility, that we may exercise our strength with wisdom
and restraint, and that we may achieve in our time and for all time
the ancient vision of 'peace on earth, good will toward men.' That
must always be our goal, and the righteousness of our cause must
always underlie our strength. For as was written long ago, 'except
the Lord keep the city, the watchman waketh but in vain.'"[3]

May 19, 1917 John Fitzgerald Kennedy is born in Brookline, Massachusetts.

1959 Oswald, now an avowed communist, defects to the Soviet Union.

1946 Kennedy enters politics as a U.S. representative from Massachusetts.

1917   1950   1960

1960 Kennedy defeats Richard Nixon in the race to become the 35th president of the United States.

1956 Oswald enlists in the U.S. Marine Corps, where he develops excellent marksmanship skills.

October 18, 1939 Lee Harvey Oswald is born in New Orleans, Louisiana.

November 22, 1963 Kennedy is assassinated while visiting Dallas, Texas, during a campaign trip. Oswald, captured just hours after the shooting, is the prime suspect.

November 24, 1963 Oswald is shot and killed by nightclub owner Jack Ruby while being transferred from Dallas police headquarters to the nearby county jail.

November 29, 1963 Succeeding president Lyndon Baines Johnson establishes the Warren Commission to formally investigate the assassination.

1962 Frustrated with Soviet life, Oswald returns to the United States along with his Russian wife, Marina.

1964 The Warren Commission presents its final report to President Johnson, concluding that Lee Harvey Oswald was Kennedy's assassin and acted alone rather than as part of a larger conspiracy.

INTRODUCTION

1. "I was in the college …" Telephone interview with Donna Macaulay, former University of Pennsylvania student, July 22, 2010.
2. "I was sitting in the barbershop having my hair cut …" Telephone interview with Walter Bartlett, former resident of Wichita, Kansas, July 25, 2010.
3. "We were in the conference room …" Dominick Dunne, in Chuck Fries (ed.) et al., We'll Never Be Young Again: Remembering the Last Days of John F. Kennedy (Beverly Hills, CA: Tallfellow Press, 2003), 3.
4. "It was a transforming moment for America …" Helen Thomas, in Vincent Bugliosi, Reclaiming History: The Assassination of President John F. Kennedy (New York: W.W. Norton, 2007), 1507.

CHAPTER ONE

1. "Take it and buy everything you …" Priscilla Johnson McMillan, Marina and Lee (New York: Harper & Row, 1977), 418.
2. "It would not be a very difficult job …" Kevin P. O'Donnell's testimony to the Warren Commission, 1964.
3. "Mr. President, they can't make you believe …" Idanell B. "Nellie" Connally's testimony to the Warren Commission, 1964.
4. "Oh no, no …" John B. Connally, Jr.'s testimony to the Warren Commission, 1964.
5. "My God, they're going to kill us …" John B. Connally, Jr.'s testimony to the Warren Commission, 1964.
6. "Oh no, no, no. Oh my God …" Jacqueline L. B. Kennedy's testimony to the Warren Commission, 1964.
7. "I kept holding the top of his head down …" Jacqueline L. B. Kennedy, in Theodore H. White, In Search of History (New York: Warner Books, 1990), 521–22.
8. "You know he's dead …" Jacqueline L. B. Kennedy, in William Manchester, The Death of a President: November 20-November 25, 1963 (New York: Harper & Row, 1967), 171.
9. "Well, it's all over …" Thomas Alexander Hutson's testimony to the Warren Commission, 1964.

CHAPTER TWO

1. "I dislike everybody." Renatus Hartogs's testimony to the Warren Commission, 1964.
2. "From everything I know about my husband …" Marina Oswald's testimony to the Warren Commission, 1964.
3. "My general impression …" Max E. Clark's testimony to the Warren Commission, 1964.
4. "A rather pleasant, appealing quality about this …" Renatus Hartogs, in Report of the Warren Commission on the Assassination of President Kennedy, New York Times Edition (New York: McGraw-Hill Book Company, 1964), 356.
5. "Defensive rigid, self-involved person …" Evelyn Siegel, in Report of the Warren Commission, 357.
6. "There are indications that he has suffered …" Evelyn Siegel, in Report of the Warren Commission, 358.
7. "I take these steps for political reasons …" Lee Harvey Oswald, in Report of the Warren Commission, 369.
8. "In the event of war …" Lee Harvey Oswald, in Report of the Warren Commission, 368.
9. "He always spoke very complimentary …" Marina Oswald's testimony to the Warren Commission, 1964.
10. "Fidel Castro needs defenders …" Lee Harvey Oswald, in Priscilla Johnson McMillan, Marina and Lee (New York: Harper & Row, 1977), 452.

CHAPTER THREE

1. "I wanted him out of office …" Robert Oswald, with Myrick and Barbara Land, Lee: A Portrait of Lee Harvey Oswald (New York: Coward-McCann, 1967), 12.
2. "I don't have to answer that …" Lee Harvey Oswald in Bugliosi, Reclaiming History, 218.
3. "Why did you bring that fool …" Lee Harvey Oswald, in Bugliosi, Reclaiming History, 223.
4. "I thought your daddy must love …" Newman R. McLarry, "My Dear Caroline," Dallas Times Herald, November 24, 1963, p. 2A.
5. "Lee, if anybody shoots at you …" James R. Leavelle on Peter Jennings Reporting: The Kennedy Assassination, Beyond Conspiracy, ABC News Special, November 20, 2003.

CHAPTER FOUR

1. "I want to splinter the CIA ..." John F. Kennedy, in L. Fletcher Prouty, JFK: The CIA, Vietnam, and the Plot to Assassinate John F. Kennedy (Secaucus, NJ: Carol Publishing, 1992), 154.
2. "Kennedy was trying to get to Castro ..." Lyndon B. Johnson, in W. J. Rorabaugh, Kennedy and the Promise of the Sixties (New York: Cambridge University Press, 2002), 223.
3. "I have no doubt that he did kill ..." Marina Oswald's testimony to the Warren Commission, 1964.
4. "Absolutely nothing ...and it's not an overnight ..." Marina Oswald on The Oprah Winfrey Show, ABC, November 22, 1996.
5. "Lee was set up as a patsy ..." Marina Oswald, in Bugliosi, Reclaiming History, 1486-7.

CHAPTER FIVE

1. "When Mr. Johnson was interrupted ..." David Kraslow, "Could It Happen Again?" Popular Science 191, no. 5 (November 1967): 73.
2. "I was working in one of the ticket booths in Penn Station ..." Telephone interview with Timothy Boyle, former Amtrak employee, July 13, 2010.
3. "We ask that we may be worthy ..." John F. Kennedy, in Suzy Platt, Respectfully Quoted: A Dictionary of Quotations (Lyndhurst, NJ: Barnes & Noble Books, 1993).

BOOKS

Engdahl, Sylvia, ed. *The John F. Kennedy Assassination*. Farmington Hills, MI: Greenhaven Press, 2010.

Harkins, Susan Sales, and William H. Harkins. *The Assassination of John F. Kennedy, 1963*. Hockessin, DE: Mitchell Lane Publishers, 2008.

Kallen, Stuart A. *The John F. Kennedy Assassination*. Farmington Hills, MI: Lucent Books, 2009.

Robson, David. *The Kennedy Assassination*. San Diego, CA: ReferencePoint Press, 2008.

Stockland, Patricia. *The Assassination of John F. Kennedy*. Edina, MN: Abdo Publishing, 2007.

DVDS

ABC News Presents: The Kennedy Assassination, Beyond Conspiracy. Koch Vision, 2004.

JFK: Three Shots That Changed America. A&E Home Video, 2010.

The Kennedy Assassination, 24 Hours After. A&E Home Video, 2010.

ON THE WEB

www.archives.gov/research/jfk/
The President John F. Kennedy Assassination Records Collection site, maintained by the United States government. Contains literally thousands of documents and images pertaining to the assassination, many of which were only recently released.

www.jfk.org
Home page of The Sixth Floor Museum at Dealey Plaza, which is located on the sixth and seventh floors of the Texas School Book Depository where most believe Oswald carried out the assassination.

www.jfk-info.com/index2.html
A privately maintained and well-organized site that offers a great deal of research material on the assassination.

http://jfklancer.com
Another privately run site with comprehensive material and up-to-the-minute news on all new developments concerning the assassination.

BOOKS

Bishop, Jim. *The Day Kennedy Was Shot*. New York: Greenwich House, 1968.

Bugliosi, Vincent. *Reclaiming History: The Assassination of President John F. Kennedy*. New York: W.W. Norton, 2007.

Douglass, James W. *JFK and the Unspeakable: Why He Died and Why It Matters*. Maryknoll, NY: Orbis Books, 2008.

Fitzpatrick, Ellen. *Letters to Jackie: Condolences from a Grieving Nation*. New York: Ecco Press, 2010.

Fries, Chuck, Spencer Green, and Irv Wilson, eds. *We'll Never Be Young Again: Remembering the Last Days of John F. Kennedy*. Beverly Hills, CA: Tallfellow Press, 2003.

Gallagher, Mary Barelli. *My Life with Jacqueline Kennedy*. Philadelphia: David McKay Company, 1969.

Hancock, Larry. *Someone Would Have Talked: The Assassination of President John F. Kennedy and the Conspiracy to Mislead History*. Southlake, TX: JFK Lancer Productions & Publications, 2006.

Hartmann, Thom, and Lamar Waldron. *Legacy of Secrecy: The Long Shadow of the JFK Assassination*. Berkeley, CA: Counterpoint Press, 2008.

Kelin, John. *Praise from a Future Generation: The Assassination of John F. Kennedy and the First Generation Critics of the Warren Report*. San Antonio, TX: Wings Press, 2007.

Lane, Mark. *Rush to Judgment*. Austin, TX: Holt, Rinehart, and Winston, 1966.

Mailer, Norman. *Oswald's Tale: An American Mystery*. New York: Random House, 1995.

Manchester, William. *The Death of a President: November 20–November 25, 1963*. New York: Harper & Row, 1967.

McDonald, Hugh C. *Appointment in Dallas: The Final Solution to the Assassination of JFK*. New York: Zebra Books, 1975.

McMillan, Priscilla Johnson. *Marina and Lee*. New York: Harper & Row, 1977.

Menninger, Bonar. *Mortal Error: The Shot That Killed JFK*. New York: St. Martin's Press, 1992.

Oswald, Robert, with Myrick and Barbara Land. *Lee: A Portrait of Lee Harvey Oswald*. New York: Coward-McCann, 1967.

Piereson, James. *Camelot and the Cultural Revolution: How the Assassination of John F. Kennedy Shattered American Liberalism*. New York: Encounter Books, 2007.

Platt, Suzy. *Respectfully Quoted: A Dictionary of Quotations*. Lyndhurst, NJ: Barnes & Noble Books, 1993.

Prouty, L. Fletcher. *JFK: The CIA, Vietnam, and the Plot to Assassinate John F. Kennedy*. Secaucus, NJ: Carol Publishing, 1992.

Report of the Warren Commission on the Assassination of President Kennedy (New York Times edition). New York: McGraw-Hill, 1964.

Rorabaugh, W. J. *Kennedy and the Promise of the Sixties*. New York: Cambridge University Press, 2002.

Scheim, David E. *Contract on America: The Mafia Murder of President John F. Kennedy*. New York: Shapolsky Publishers, 1988.

Sneed, Larry A. *No More Silence: An Oral History of the Assassination of President Kennedy*. Dallas, TX: Three Forks Press, 1998.

White, Theodore H. *In Search of History*. New York: Warner Books, 1990.

ARTICLES

Kraslow, David. "Could It Happen Again?" *Popular Science* 191, no. 5 (November 1967): 70–73, 194–198.

McLarry, Newman R. "My Dear Caroline." *Dallas Times Herald*, November 24, 1963, p. 2A.

PERSONAL INTERVIEWS

Telephone interview with Walter Bartlett, former resident of Wichita, Kansas, July 25, 2010.

Telephone interview with Timothy Boyle, former Amtrak employee, July 13, 2010.

Telephone interview with Donna Macaulay, former University of Pennsylvania student, July 22, 2010.

TELEVISION INTERVIEWS

Leavelle, James R. *Peter Jennings Reporting: The Kennedy Assassination, Beyond Conspiracy*. ABC News Special, November 20, 2003.

Oswald, Marina. *The Oprah Winfrey Show*, ABC, November 22, 1996.

COURT TESTIMONIES

Clark, Max E. Testimony given to the Warren Commission, 1964.

Connally, Idanell B. "Nellie." Testimony given to the Warren Commission, 1964.

Connally, Jr., John B. Testimony given to the Warren Commission, 1964.

Crawford, James N. Testimony given to the Warren Commission, 1964.

Hartogs, Renatus. Testimony given to the Warren Commission, 1964.

Hutson, Thomas Alexander. Testimony given to the Warren Commission, 1964.

Kennedy, Jacqueline L. B. Testimony given to the Warren Commission, 1964.

O'Donnell, Kevin P. Testimony given to the Warren Commission, 1964.

Oswald, Marina. Testimony given to the Warren Commission, 1964.

INDEX

ABOUT THE AUTHOR

Wil Mara is the award-winning author of more than 140 books. He has written fiction and nonfiction for both children and adults. More information about his work can be found at www.wilmara.com.